Oceans and Seas

Diyan Leake

Raintree is an imprint of Capstone Global Library Limited, a company incorporated in England and Wales having its registered office at 7 Pilgrim Street, London, EC4V 6LB – Registered company number: 6695582

www.raintreepublishers.co.uk
myorders@raintreepublishers.co.uk

Edited by Joanna Issa and Penny West
Designed by Philippa Jenkins
Original illustrations © Capstone Global Library Ltd 2014
Picture research by Mica Brancic
Production by Helen McCreath
Originated by Capstone Global Library Ltd
Printed and bound in China

ISBN 978 1 406 28386 0
18 17 16 15 14
10 9 8 7 6 5 4 3 2 1

British Library Cataloguing in Publication Data
Leake, Diyan
        Oceans and Seas (Water, Water Everywhere!)
A full catalogue record for this book is available from the British Library.

Acknowledgements
We would like to thank the following for permission to reproduce photographs: Alamy pp. 5 (© mark ferguson), 15, 23b (© F1online digitale Bildagentur GmbH), 17 (© Eugene Senada), 18 (© Gunter Marx / HA), 19, 23c (© Peter Fakler), 22c (© Arco Images GmbH); Getty Images pp. 14 (Oxford Scientific), 20 (Huw Jones); Shutterstock pp. 4 (© Iakov Kalinin), 6, 7, 22b, 23a (© Stephen Rees), 9 (© InnaFelker), 10 (© windu), 12 (© worldswildlifewonders), 13 (© Kuttelvaserova Stuchelova), 16 (© Gerard van Hemeren), 22a (© Nejron Photo), 21 (age fotostock/David Page).

Cover photograph reproduced with permission of Shutterstock (© EpicStockMedia).
Back cover photograph reproduced with permission of Shutterstock/© InnaFelker.

We would like to thank Michael Bright and Diana Bentley for their invaluable help in the preparation of this book.

Contents

Oceans

An ocean is a very big body of water.

coast

The land at the edge of an ocean is called the coast.

There can be a beach by
the ocean.

A beach is where the land goes down to the ocean.

Oceans of the world

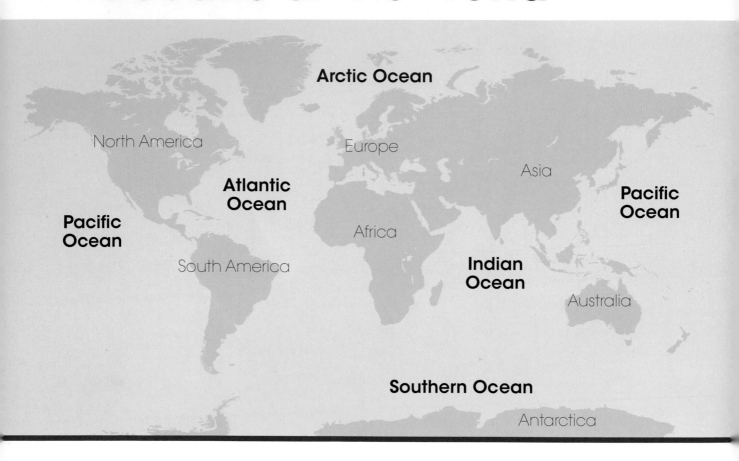

Arctic Ocean

North America

Europe

Asia

Atlantic
Ocean

Pacific
Ocean

Pacific
Ocean

Africa

Indian
Ocean

South America

Australia

Southern Ocean

Antarctica

There are five oceans on Earth.

This is the Atlantic Ocean.

Seas of the world

A sea is like an ocean but it is smaller.

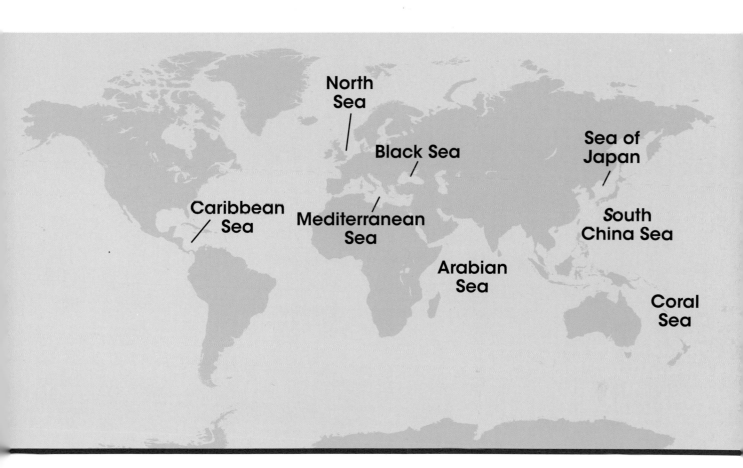

There are many seas on Earth.

Living things in the ocean

Seaweed looks like a plant and grows in the sea.

Sometimes there is seaweed
on the beach.

Shells are the homes of some
animals that live in the ocean.

Sometimes there are shells on the beach.

Fishing in the ocean

People go out on the ocean in fishing boats.

People catch fish in the salty
water of the ocean.

Waves on the ocean

An ocean can be stormy.

Wind blows over the water and makes big waves.

Having fun by the ocean

It is fun to spend time by the ocean.

Stay safe! Always have an adult with you when you are near water.

Quiz

Which of these shows an ocean?

A

B

C

Answer on page 24

Picture glossary

 **beach** sandy or pebbly area where the land goes down to the ocean or sea

 **shell** hard covering that some sea animals have around them to keep them safe

 **waves** the movement of water in the ocean caused by the wind

Index

Answer to quiz on page 22: Picture **B** shows the ocean.

Note to parents and teachers

Before reading
Collect a few items associated with the seaside (e.g. a shell, some smooth pebbles, and a plastic bucket and spade). Show the children the items, explaining you brought them back from a place you visited recently, and asking the children to guess where you went. On a globe or a map of the world point out the location of the place you 'visited'. Demonstrate how the sea in this location is part of the huge area of water that covers most of the Earth. Introduce the term 'ocean'.

After reading
• Help the children to find out more about some of the plants and animals that live in the ocean. Together, they could make a collage of sealife, using lots of different media.
• Encourage the children to create their own 'ocean motions' by mimicking the movements of ocean animals that you have discussed.